DIGITAL AND INFORMATION LITERACY ™

WIKIPEDIA, 3.5 MILLION ARTICLES & COUNTING

USING AND ASSESSING THE PEOPLE'S ENCYCLOPEDIA

HEATHER HASAN

rosen publishing's
rosen
central®

New York

To my nephew, Chase—You are such a joy.

Published in 2012 by The Rosen Publishing Group, Inc.
29 East 21st Street, New York, NY 10010

First Edition

Library of Congress Cataloging-in-Publication Data

Hasan, Heather.
Wikipedia, 3.5 million articles and counting: using and assessing the people's encyclopedia/Heather Hasan.—1st ed.
    p. cm.—(Digital and information literacy)
Includes bibliographical references and index.
ISBN 978-1-4488-5557-5 (library binding)—
ISBN 978-1-4488-5620-6 (pbk.)—
ISBN 978-1-4488-5622-0 (6-pack)
1. Wikipedia—Juvenile literature. 2. Electronic encyclopedias—Juvenile literature.
3. Wikis (Computer science)—Juvenile literature. 4. User-generated content—Juvenile
literature. I. Title. II. Title: Wikipedia, three point five million articles and counting.
AE100.H37 2012
030—dc23

2011028510

Manufactured in the United States of America

CPSIA Compliance Information: Batch #W12YA: For further information, contact Rosen Publishing, New York, New York, at 1-800-237-9932.

CONTENTS

INTRODUCTION

An encyclopedia is a reference work that contains information on a wide range of subjects. Currently, Wikipedia is the largest encyclopedia in the world. Over 17 million articles are found in more than 280 languages throughout its pages. Over 3.5 million articles are written in English, and this number increases every day. Every day, thousands of users from around the world collectively create thousands of new articles for this massive online encyclopedia. The English version alone has over fourteen million people registered to use it.

However, Wikipedia is like no other encyclopedia that has come before it. This encyclopedia is not found on paper and is not bound within a book. Instead, Wikipedia uses the concept of wikis—a technology that allows for the collaborative creation of Web sites—to develop, build, and maintain an online encyclopedia. It does not pay experts in their fields to write it, but relies on everyday users to make entries. It does not even pay experts to review the amateur-written articles, but again looks to its users to fact-check and edit the content. Unlike any encyclopedia that came before it, Wikipedia is also free for people to use, copy, edit, and distribute. Anyone with Internet access can contribute and make changes to a Wikipedia article. Its editors come from all over the world and sometimes provide information that would not be found in traditional Western publications.

Wikipedia's articles are often the first that appear when Internet users do Google searches. These articles can be very useful in aiding a user's research.

Wikipedia's unique qualities give it both the ability to be an asset to a researcher as well as a detriment. It can be useful in getting users started in their research and leading them to other, more reputable, and expert-written and -reviewed sources. However, caution should be taken when using Wikipedia. Because its content is free for anyone to use, write, and edit, it can contain information that is false. This book will examine the history and philosophy of Wikipedia, how this revolutionary encyclopedia works, how it is policed and maintained, and how users can safely and responsibly use it as a research tool.

The History and Philosophy of Wikipedia

The idea for a free, online encyclopedia originated with Jimmy Wales, an American Internet entrepreneur. Wales wanted his encyclopedia to be licensed as free content. This means that the information on the Web site would be free for everyone to access, copy, alter, and distribute. Wales, who had started a dot-com called Bomis in 1996, called his online encyclopedia project Nupedia.

The Precursor: Nupedia

In early 2000, Wales recruited a philosophy student named Larry Sanger to lead the online encyclopedia project. Wales and Sanger had originally met in online forums discussing philosophy and objectivism. Objectivism expresses the idea that reality exists independently of human consciousness, but can be perceived accurately through the senses, conceptual thinking, and logic. According to this philosophy, even human values and knowledge exist independently of humans and are discovered, not created, by our

Jimmy Wales is both the cofounder and promoter of the popular online encyclopedia Wikipedia.

thought. Objectivism also insists upon the absolute rights of the individual, including his or her right to attempt to reproduce reality through a free expression of his or her ideas.

Wales wanted the Nupedia project to put the theory of objectivism into practice. In Sanger's words, "Neutrality, we agreed, required that articles should not represent any one point of view on controversial subjects, but instead fairly represent all sides" (as quoted by Larry Sanger in the article "Open Sources 2.0"). The free mingling of ideas in this kind of forum would, theoretically, allow for a closer approach to objective reality.

Sanger was given the freedom to explore different ways to design the Nupedia project. He felt strongly that the volunteer authors and editors of Nupedia's articles should be experts in their fields. While the definition of an expert author allowed for some flexibility, Sanger felt that editors should be true authorities, possessing (with few exceptions) a Ph.D. in relevant disciplines. The role of the editors would be to assign topics to the writers and to oversee the editorial process. In Sanger's vision, a top-down structure like this was needed in order to maintain quality.

Embracing the Wiki Ideal

Wales used his company, Bomis, to fund Nupedia, with the idea of eventually generating revenue by selling advertising on the site. When Bomis's revenues began to drop, Wales looked for a way to produce his encyclopedia without having to pay anyone. To save even more money, he sought to abbreviate or eliminate altogether the lengthy review process that each article underwent before being released to the public. The Nupedia editorial process was a rigorous one, consisting of seven steps during which a document was reviewed and copyedited several times. The experts were expensive, and the editorial process was so slow and deliberate that it was not producing enough content.

Wales and his team liked the idea of allowing the general public to draft articles and offer "open review" comments on the content's accuracy and objectivity. However, Nupedia needed to find a way to more readily

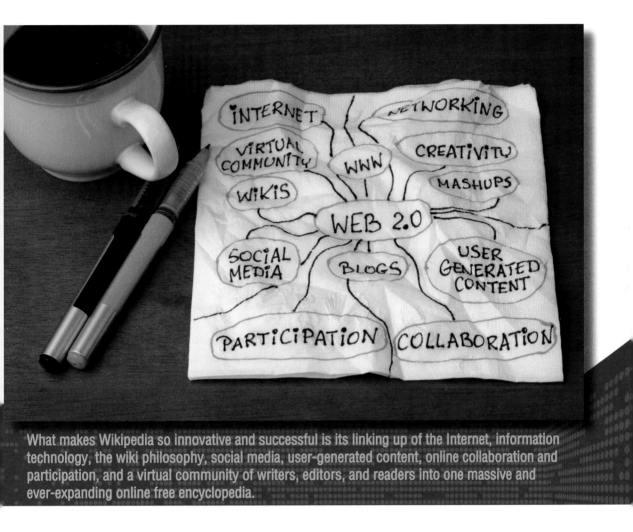

What makes Wikipedia so innovative and successful is its linking up of the Internet, information technology, the wiki philosophy, social media, user-generated content, online collaboration and participation, and a virtual community of writers, editors, and readers into one massive and ever-expanding online free encyclopedia.

invite the participation of ordinary, uncredentialed people. It was very difficult to get amateur-written articles through Nupedia's elaborate expert-review system. This is when the Nupedia team came across Howard (Ward) Cunningham and the idea of wikis.

A wiki is a Web site that allows the creation and editing of interlinked Web pages. Wikis are often used to create collaborative works. This means that different users can enter information into a Web page stored within a common database. Wikis can have dozens or thousands of different people adding their expertise to a Web page. Wiki technology was developed by Cunningham. A computer programmer, Cunningham developed WikiWikiWeb, a system in which all changes to the content on a Web page occur by simply pressing an "edit" button. The name "wiki" comes from a Hawaiian word for "fast."

Sanger and Wales decided to apply Cunningham's wiki technology to Nupedia's inefficient collaborative system and its extremely slow pace of article generation. This side-project was named Wikipedia, a combination of the words "wiki" and "encyclopedia." In January 2001, Wikipedia was first introduced. It was initially designed to complement, not compete with, Nupedia. Wikipedia was meant to serve as a source of articles to feed into Nupedia.

The Emergence of Wikipedia

Wikipedia started as a side project to Nupedia, allowing for collaboration on articles prior to the beginning of the expert review process. At first, the plan was for Nupedia to continue in its role of editing and expert reviewing all articles, even those generated by Wikipedia and its amateur authors. Though Wikipedia was originally launched to complement Nupedia's efforts and supply it with content, it quickly surpassed its predecessor in popularity. As Wikipedia became more and more successful, it required more and more attention. The inefficient, content-starved Nupedia began to suffer from neglect.

In 2002, Bomis could no longer pay Sanger, who then left both the Nupedia and Wikipedia projects. Soon after that, in 2003, Nupedia was abandoned completely. Wikipedia, however, was thriving. By the end of its first month (January 2001), it already had about six hundred articles. By March of that year, it had 1,300 articles. By April, it had grown to 2,300, and by May, 3,900 articles had been submitted. At the end of its first year of existence, over twenty thousand encyclopedia entries had been created. Wikipedia was growing exponentially, by leaps and bounds. In contrast, thousands of experts had volunteered articles in the three years following Nupedia's launch. Yet its lengthy and involved review process resulted in the

"WIKI WIKI"

"Wiki Wiki"

Ward Cunningham came up with the name for his WikiWikiWeb in 1982, when he and his wife were on their honeymoon in Hawaii. An airport agent told him to take the "Wiki Wiki." In Hawaiian, the word *wiki* means "quick," and *wiki wiki* means "super quick." Apparently, the Wiki Wiki was the shuttle bus at the airport that transported people quickly between terminals. Cunningham found this word perfect for his new creation.

completion of only twenty-four completed, edited, and posted articles by the time the project was abandoned in September 2003.

Open Source, Rapid Growth

One of the reasons why Wikipedia grew in popularity and size so quickly was because of its nature as an open-source encyclopedia. From the beginning, the open content license of Wikipedia allowed for the copying, modification, and distribution of its works. It also required that any of the modified versions of those works also retain these rights. In other words, the content on Wikipedia is free. Users are free to use it, study it, modify it, and copy and share it with others. The idea that their work would be free for others to read motivated contributors to add to the site from the very start. In the eyes of Wikipedia contributors, the online encyclopedia gave them an opportunity to reach a vast audience they would never be able to access otherwise. As a result, this allowed them to teach the world about what they knew and share what they believed to be crucially important knowledge.

Wikipedia's openness and ease of editing also made it easy for new users to join and start editing right away. Wikipedia allowed anyone to contribute to the site. Unlike Nupedia, all contributors were welcome. No

Wikipedia's main page, shown here, offers links to current news articles, "On this day..." items, and a daily featured picture and article.

one was turned away for not being educated enough or a good enough writer. After all, any weaknesses in an article's content could always be fixed or shored up by the next contributor.

The fact that, from the beginning, unedited works were added to Wikipedia, later to be refined through user collaboration, also helped it to get underway and quickly take off. Wikipedia encourages users to add their unfinished works to the site, with the idea that the works will improve through the successive contributions of others. This collaboration allows for a work to move forward quickly, as it is not reliant on the time-consuming refinement and revisions of a single author and editor. This fact helped Wikipedia grow quickly and maintain a steady flow of incoming content.

Though Nupedia did not ultimately succeed, it started Wikipedia off with a good core group of people who understood what an online, user-generated encyclopedia should be. They set a precedent for Wikipedia and helped the project develop a functional, cooperative, serious-minded, and committed community of contributors.

Chapter 2

How Wikipedia Works

Wikipedia works like a traditional encyclopedia, except that its articles appear online and for free and are written and edited by amateurs. With a traditional encyclopedia, the publisher pays an expert to write an article on a given subject. With Wikipedia, however, articles can be written by anyone. The article can then be edited, corrected, and revised by any user. The content on Wikipedia is created strictly by its users. Contributors do not have to be academics or professionals working in the field about which they are writing.

Wikipedia's Core Policies

Early on, three core policies regarding content emerged for Wikipedia. These were: Neutral Point of View (NPOV), Verification (V), and No Original Research (NOR). Together, these policies gauge what type of material is acceptable in a Wikipedia article and set a standard for the quality of the information found in it.

Before creating an article or contributing to an already-written one, users should be aware of these policies. Wikipedia's neutrality reflects its

WIKIPEDIA

English
The Free Encyclopedia
3 560 000+ articles

日本語
フリー百科事典
734 000+ 記事

Español
La enciclopedia li
702 000+ articles

Deutsch
Die freie Enzyklopädie
1 190 000+ Artikel

Français
encyclopédie libre
386 000+ articles

Русский
Свободная энц
80 000+

Italiano
L' enciclopedia libera
774 000+ voci

Português
A enciclopédi
670 000+

Nederlands
De vrije encyclopedie
672 000+ artikelen

Polski
Wolna encyklopedia
775 000+ haseł

sukai · ricerca · 検索 · buscar · busca · zoeken
cesés · tim kiếm · căutare · 報尋 · Пошук

Wikipedia articles are written in over 280 languages. Wikipedia's logo, shown here, represents this fact by featuring a puzzle globe with alphabetic characters from many different languages.

commitment to avoid advocating only one point of view. Authors and editors should strive for accuracy and objectivity above all else and not allow their personal feelings or views to enter into the writing.

All Wikipedia articles should also be verifiable. References to sources must always be provided. If verifiable, authoritative references are not given for content provided by a contributor, that content may be removed from the Wikipedia site. Therefore, any key information should be followed by a footnote. The footnote is actually a link to the references section of the article, where there is a complete list of citations. By clicking the footnote, a user would be taken directly to these citations, which are made up of books, academic papers, magazine articles, and Web sites.

Citations are important because they allow users to quickly and easily see where certain information came from and to decide whether or not that information came from a reliable source. Citations are also useful in helping a user find additional information on a subject. Many of the source names within a citation provide links to the source online. If a source is not available online, a user would have to find it at a library or bookstore.

The Five Pillars

The fundamental principles by which Wikipedia operates can be summarized in the form of five "pillars." These are:

1. Wikipedia is an online encyclopedia.
2. Wikipedia has a neutral point of view.
3. Wikipedia is free content.
4. Wikipedians should interact in a respectful and civil manner.
5. Wikipedia does not have firm rules.

The significance of Wikipedia's No Original Research (NOR) policy is related to the importance it places on citations and verification. All content in Wikipedia entries must be attributed to a reliable information source. Content cannot simply be created by a contributor off the top of his or her head and backed up by nothing but opinion and fabricated facts and statistics. Information that appears in a Wikipedia article must be derived from already-published work. An author's original research or thoughts are not welcome. The contributor must be able to provide a source outside of himself or herself for every fact and concept that appears in a Wikipedia article.

Creating a Wikipedia Entry

Anyone can write an article for Wikipedia. Sometimes articles are written in their entirety before being posted. Other times they begin as "stubs" and eventually grow into complete and thorough articles through the additions and enhancements of successive contributors. Article stubs can start out as short as a few sentences. Then other people with knowledge on the subject or who are willing to research the topic can come along and add to its content.

The steps one must follow to write an article for Wikipedia are relatively few and easy. Anyone can simply go to Wikipedia's main page or, to write in a language other than English, visit its international page. Before beginning to write, a contributor should first check to see if an article already exists on the particular subject about which he or she wishes to write. With more than 3.5 million English-language articles in Wikipedia, one might think that every conceivable topic has already been covered, but this is not the case. If no article exists on a certain subject, a user is free to write about it. To contribute an article, a user must first register with and log on to the Wikipedia Web site. Then, the article would be written in an editing box. Once the "save page" button is clicked, the article has been added to the Wikipedia site.

Articles should be devoted to topics that are worthy of inclusion in traditional print encyclopedias. They should be of general and broad interest, something that a lot of people would be compelled to read. An article also

It is fairly easy for anyone to add an article to Wikipedia or edit an existing article. In the true wiki spirit, writing and editing an article can even be a collaborative effort.

needs to be verifiable, with references to books, magazines, journals, and Web sites that address the same subject and that have been used to provide the information found in the Wikipedia entry. Wikipedia articles should never reflect the bias or opinions of the author. Therefore, contributors should strive to represent all sides of an issue, question, debate, or controversy equally and fairly.

The structure of a standard Wikipedia article includes a summary, a table of contents, sections and section headings, images, citations, and appendixes. The summary, or lead section, of an article is just a short intro-duction. Wikipedia displays a table of contents between the summary and the first section heading. The table of contents is created automatically by Wikipedia as sections are added within the article.

Wikipedia offers many different ways to format the text of any article. Most of the formatting is accomplished by surrounding the text with some sort of code. For example, a section heading is formatted by putting equal signs on either side of the heading text like this: ==Heading==. Appropriate images, such as photographs, maps, drawings, or graphs can be uploaded and inserted into an article as long as they are in the public domain or the contributor has secured the rights to reproduce or otherwise use them.

Sources for the key information in an article also need to be cited. Footnotes are inserted into the relevant text. The source for this footnoted information is then listed in the article's "reference" section. Some Wikipedia articles also contain appendixes. These may include references that provide additional notes about the main text, a bibliography that provides a list of related books and articles, a "see also" section that lists related Wikipedia articles, or an "external links" section that provides links to other pages relat-ing to the subject that can be found elsewhere on the Web.

The Watchlist

Wikipedia articles are constantly being modified. If users wish to be notified when a particular article of interest has been edited, they can subscribe to an article's watchlist. Any logged-in user has the ability to keep a list of "watched" pages (such as ones he or she has written or edited), which can be accessed by clicking on a "My Watchlist" link found at the top of any Wikipedia page. Because of this feature, not many acts of vandalism against a page will go unnoticed for long.

Editing a Wikipedia Article

If an article about a particular subject already exists, a contributor can add to, or edit, the existing article. By clicking on the "view source" tab at the upper right-hand side of a given article page, and then clicking the "edit" tab, any user can simply make changes directly to the text of any unprotected article. Though an account is needed to create an article from scratch, users do not need to open an account to edit an article. However, if an account is not created before editing an article, the contributor's IP address would be recorded publicly on the page's edit history. If an account is created, a user's IP address can be concealed.

Users who are new to Wikipedia can practice writing and editing in the sandbox. After the text is typed, the user can click on "show preview" to test changes or "save page" when he or she is happy with the way it looks.

Because Wikipedia is a user-edited encyclopedia, almost any given article can be edited by any user at any time. However, Wikipedia keeps a history of every version of every article on its site. The edits made to a particular article can be viewed by clicking the "view history" tab at the top right of a page. This page contains all of the old versions of an article, shows the date and time of the edits made to the article, and lists the username or IP address of the person who made each particular edit.

Wikipedia encourages its users to be bold and unafraid to edit other writers' work. This reflects the idea that each new user may find something in an article that can be improved upon, such as spelling, grammar, readability, accuracy, or quality of content. However, an article may not always be changed for the better. Sometimes inaccurate information is added, a user will purposely deface an article with nonsense or gibberish, or a contributor may delete factual information that he or she disagrees with or that undermines his or her pet theories. For this reason, it is very useful that every version of a particular article is saved in its entirety under the "view history" tab. Edits can always be reversed, fixed, or improved upon later by other Wikipedians.

For those users who have never before contributed to a Wikipedia article, there is a Wikipedia help page to get them started. Here, users can learn how to perform such tasks as formatting, creating links, footnoting, and adding public domain images. Before actually writing or editing an article, a user can experiment on Wikipedia's sandbox page. In the sandbox, users can practice writing or editing and can become familiar with the Wikipedia formatting codes. The changes that the user makes in the sandbox will not be permanent. The sandbox page is "wiped clean" every twelve hours.

Chapter 3

Policing and Improving Wikipedia Entries

hen Wikipedia was first launched, it had few, if any, rules. The focus was on getting as many articles written and developed as quickly as possible. It was far less concerned with determining who would be considered qualified to add to the wiki. Though the Wikipedia community cherishes the fact that it is free and open, its users also want it to remain peaceful and reliable as well. Therefore, throughout Wikipedia's history, polices and positions have been developed to promote such ideals.

Wikipedia's Management System

Administrators are Wikipedia editors who have been entrusted with access to certain technical features, or tools. Administrators have the ability, among other things, to block certain users from editing articles, to control page protection, and to delete problematic pages. These are actions that can impact the entire Wikipedia site, and administrators are expected to exhibit a high

Sue Gardner is the executive director of the Wikimedia Foundation, a nonprofit organization that operates several online collaborative wiki projects in addition to Wikipedia.

standard of conduct. They are to use the tools fairly, never for personal motivation or gain. Presently, there are about 1,800 administrators in the Wikipedia community.

There are no official prerequisites for becoming an administrator, except that the editor must have an account and a basic level of trust from other editors. Any user may nominate another user or himself or herself for the position. Nominations remain posted for a week, during which time users can give their opinions and ask questions. At the end of the week, a bureaucrat reviews the discussion to see if most users agree with the nomination. Bureaucrats are Wikipedia users with the ability to promote other users to the status of administrator or bureaucrat, grant or revoke an account's bot status, or rename a user's account. If an administrator abuses his or her administrative powers, these powers can be revoked.

The power to revoke an administrator or bureaucrat's rights belongs to stewards, a small, multilingual group of Wikipedians who are elected and reconfirmed annually. These powers can also be removed by Wales or by a ruling of the Arbitration Committee. Arbitrators are volunteer users, usually experienced editors and administrators, who are elected by the Wikipedia community.

File   Edit   View   Favorites   Tools   Help

WIKIPEDIA'S ROBOTS

Wikipedia's Robots

Wikipedia robots (or bots) were created to insert data into Wikipedia much like a human editor would but far faster. These software programs, created by Wikipedians, are designed to reformat pages and fix punctuation, but there are also bots that can create articles and load numbers from databases. Bots are registered under special bot accounts so that they can be easily distinguished from their human counterparts.

Edit Wars and the Three-Revert Rule

As Wikipedia grew, editors often began to cross paths while working on the same article. Sometimes they disagreed about the article's content and how it should be altered. One user would change a word from an article, and another user would change it back. Then, the first user would revert it again.

In Wikipedia, a revert is simply undoing the work of another user. Reverts are intended to be used to undo vandalism or to correct a small mistake made by another user. They are not meant to be used by dueling editors, each fighting for his or her preferred version of an article to win out. Though Wikipedia encourages its users to be bold, it does not find such exchanges—dubbed "edit wars"—to be productive. Edit wars occur when

Wikipedia's various rules, which include the prohibiting of personal attacks, harassment, edit wars, and vandalism, were established to help administrators maintain a spirit of civility among the online encyclopedia's users and contributors.

both sides determine that they are right and will not yield or compromise with each other. Edit wars have broken out over anything from the use of a single word to the treatment of a whole topic.

To counter such edit wars, Wikipedia's users have developed the "Three-Revert Rule." This rule states that an editor should not undo someone else's edits to an article more than three times per day. Talk pages (also known as discussion pages), in which editors can discuss improvements to an article or ask questions about edits, are designed to quell such arguments. Discussion page tabs are found at the upper left of each article page. It is hoped that, through civil discussion, editors will be able to come to some sort of consensus and avoid drawn-out conflict or all-out edit wars. Breaking the Three-Revert Rule is considered an act of hostility within the Wikipedia community and will result in a user being blocked from editing on the site.

The Tools of an Administrator: Blocking, Deleting, and Protecting

Administrators have the power to block users, thereby preventing them from editing Wikipedia articles. Blocks are usually temporary, lasting a few days or months, and come only after the user has been warned several times.

Blocks are intended to prevent damage or disruption to Wikipedia. Blocks are imposed in response to behavior such as vandalism, gross incivility, harassment, spamming, violating Wikipedia polices, or threatening another user. Vandalism is considered anything from illegitimately making pages blank to adding obscenities to a page or writing nonsense into an article. Wikipedians are expected to treat each other with consideration and respect. If a user's incivility rises to the level of disruptiveness, personal attacks against another user, harassment, or threatening behavior, that user may also be blocked. Blatant acts of advertising, or spamming, on the Wikipedia site can also provide grounds for an administrator to block a user.

Administrators have the power to delete pages from Wikipedia that do not meet the encyclopedia's criteria for content. These articles may contain copyright violations or vandalism. They may lack proper verification,

Shane Fitzgerald, shown here in his home in Dublin, Ireland, posted a phony quote on Wikipedia to test how well the site would identify and correct any errors. Wikipedia passed the test – the false quote was recognized and removed by Wikipedia's administrators.

citations, and sourcing. The subject matter may not be deemed notable or of wide and general interest. If an administrator feels that an article cannot be edited to remedy any of these flaws, he or she has the ability to delete the current article and all its previous versions from public view. Roughly five thousand pages are deleted from Wikipedia in this way each day.

Administrators are also able to protect an article in order to restrict the editing of that page. Articles can be semiprotected or fully protected. Indefinite semiprotection prevents unregistered Wikipedia users and new users from making changes to articles that are prone to vandalism. Fully protected pages can only be edited by administrators. This tool is used on pages that are experiencing edit wars. A temporary full protection blocks anyone from editing the page until the parties have discussed their edits on the talk page and have reached a consensus. An administrator can remove a protection from a page if the reason for the protection no longer applies.

MYTHS & FACTS

MYTH Wikipedia has no value whatsoever and should never be used.

FACT Wikipedia is useful when used as a starting point for research. The bulk of one's research, however, should be drawn from primary sources and long-established, reputable information sources—both print and digital—that rely on expert writing and reviewing of content. The sources that a Wikipedia article cites may be more valuable works to consult as you expand your research.

MYTH Wikipedia is always reliable and accurate.

FACT Wikipedia articles can be accurate. Because of their open content policy, however, they cannot be trusted to always provide fact-checked, verified, expert-supplied and -reviewed information.

MYTH Wikipedia is generally accepted as a reputable source for use and citation in formal research projects and papers.

FACT Most teachers do not find Wikipedia articles to be acceptable reference material for research projects and papers. Wikipedia should be used to get some general background information on a subject before consulting more substantial, advanced, and reputable expert-written and -reviewed sources (both print and online).

Chapter 4

Using Wikipedia Wisely

ikipedia is set apart from other encyclopedias in that it is free for everyone to use and is open to anyone to edit. This openness results in both Wikipedia's strengths and its weaknesses. Though Wikipedia can be a great tool for beginning to learn about and research a topic, not everything found on Wikipedia is accurate, comprehensive, or unbiased. Therefore, students relying on Wikipedia as a resource in their research and writing process should do so with care.

Wikipedia's Weaknesses

The ideal Wikipedia article is neutral, balanced, and encyclopedic (thorough, detailed, and complete). It should contain notable and verifiable information. This is not always the case, however. Unlike traditional encyclopedias, Wikipedia has no formal expert-review process. It is a self-policing project. A scientific or medical article, therefore, will not only be written by an amateur (most likely), but it will also not necessarily have an expert scientist or medical professional reviewing and editing it.

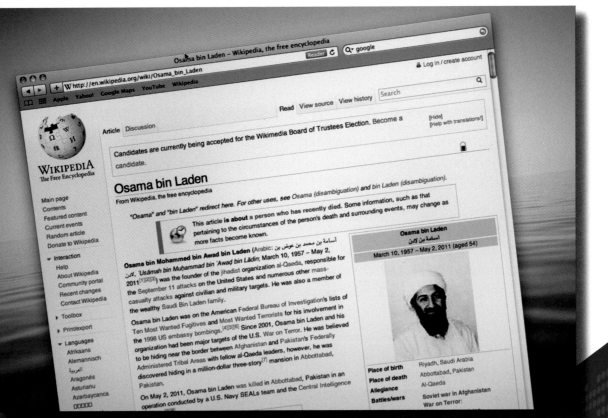

Being Web-based and having a very large number of active writers allow Wikipedia to provide rapidly updated coverage of many topics, including subjects that are affected by breaking news. It also allows for hyperlinking to other information sources—a feature that is unavailable in traditional media.

Though the information in a Wikipedia article may be generally correct, it may also contain misleading information or information that is just plain wrong. It is possible for misinformation to creep into an article and for that misinformation to go unnoticed by Wikipedia's editors. Because anyone can edit Wikipedia, the site is also prone to vandalism. Though administrative tools make it easy to quickly eliminate vandalism, a student can unknowingly be viewing a vandalized page before any administrator notices the problem.

File   Edit   View   Favorites   Tools   Help

WIKIPEDIA GETS IT WRONG: THE CASE OF JOHN SEIGENTHALER

Wikipedia Gets It Wrong: The Case of John Seigenthaler

John Seigenthaler, a retired journalist and former editorial page editor at the national newspaper *USA Today*, founded the Freedom Forum First Amendment Center at Vanderbilt University. He was also Robert F. Kennedy's administrative assistant in the early 1960s. On May 26, 2005, a false biography of Seigenthaler was posted on Wikipedia that depicted him as a suspect in the assassinations of both Kennedy and his brother, U.S. President John F. Kennedy. This act of vandalism and misinformation remained on Wikipedia's Web site for 132 days before it was removed. Because their computers were programmed to copy data verbatim from Wikipedia, Reference.com and Answers.com also posted the same scandalous and libelous information.

Though misinformation and vandalism on Wikipedia are usually corrected fairly quickly, intentional and unintentional errors can sometimes linger for months and spread throughout the Internet. This is evidenced by the long-standing, defamatory Wikipedia article about prominent journalist John Seigenthaler *(pictured here)*.

Wikipedia has a very large contributor base. These contributors come from diverse backgrounds and share a wide range of opinions. Because numerous editors help shape and craft each article, Wikipedia entries, in theory, eventually achieve a state of neutrality, reflecting no one viewpoint. Yet this process may take a very long time. This is especially true for controversial topics. An editor writing from a certain point of view may present one side of an issue, while barely mentioning the other. Editors may also emphasize the elements of a topic that support their view, while ignoring those that refute or undermine it.

After an article concerning a controversial topic has been edited by several users, it may contain a confusing combination of conflicting facts. This reflects the various editors' clashing viewpoints, selective use of information, and bias. This hodgepodge of information, fact, and opinion can be very confusing for students and can render the article's content unusable for research purposes. Wikipedia articles ideally improve over time through the editing process. However, users should be aware that, when they view any given article, it could be in any stage of the editing process. Not all articles are of encyclopedic quality from the start.

Because Wikipedia articles can vary greatly in quality, factuality, and trustworthiness, it is not wise to use Wikipedia as the sole source for a research paper or report. In fact, most educational institutions do not consider Wikipedia to be a proper, citable source at all.

A Good Starting Point: The Merits of Wikipedia

Wikipedia is intended to be a starting point in the research process, not an end point. It is useful when a person is just beginning to dig for information on a topic. Links within articles allow users to pursue interesting and related topic threads. Any blue text found within an article is actually a link to another related Wikipedia entry.

Other relevant articles can be found at the bottom of a Wikipedia article in the "see also" section. Clicking on any of the links found there

Though Wikipedia can be a good starting point in the research process, it is still important for students to utilize sources that are considered to be more reliable by teachers and professors. These include reputable books and newspaper and magazine articles.

will lead the user to the full article. Another useful technique for researching with Wikipedia is the "What Links Here" feature. This link appears on the left side of the page as the first item in the box marked "Toolbox." "What Links Here" gives the user a complete list of other Wikipedia articles that link and are related to the article at hand. Following links such as these can give a researcher a broader understanding of his or her topic and access to higher-quality information sources. In this way, the information contained in a Wikipedia article can be used as a launching point for further research. A user can take the facts found in a Wikipedia article, verify them with other sources, and use them to flesh out a good paper.

Examining an article's history and discussion pages can also help a user become more familiar with the topic at hand. Reading an article's history and talk pages can give a researcher insight into which facts are under dispute and can also help him or her decide what information may merit further research and external verification.

Wikipedia can also serve as a great guide to additional resources that are considered to be more credible by teachers, librarians, and other academics. There are several places within a Wikipedia article that link to often more reputable, non-Wikipedia information sources. Good Wikipedia editors get their information from external (outside) sources and document them in an article's reference and bibliography sections. Many articles also contain further reading sections and external links sections. These sections are found at the bottom of an article's page and often contain links to newspaper articles, books, or other Web-based sources.

What to Look for When Using Wikipedia

The most accurate Wikipedia articles are well-sourced. Therefore, it is wise for a researcher to check an article's reference and bibliography sections when using Wikipedia. However, many articles contain statements that are not fully cited. If an article has very few references, a user has no way of knowing if the information it contains has come from reliable sources. Sometimes a sparsely referenced article will even have a note at the top of the page that states, "This article needs additional citations for verification." A user should be wary of articles that list only a single source or that list multiple sources that all ultimately derive from a single source. If an article does provide sources, a user should access these sources to be sure that they actually support what the article is saying.

Another way to recognize more reliable articles is to look for ones that display small bronze stars in their upper-right corners. These articles are

Many students, such as this Boston University graduate, are grateful for Wikipedia and its usefulness and convenience as a tool for research.

considered "featured articles." They have undergone a broad, systematic review by editors and have been deemed to be of high quality in the areas of neutrality, accuracy, completeness, and style. The second-best tier of articles is designated "good articles." These articles have also been deemed to be well-written, accurate, neutral, and verifiable, but they have not yet reached featured article quality. A list of featured articles and good articles can be found under the "featured articles" link found in the box marked "featured content" on the left side of any Wikipedia page. Featured articles usually remain at a high quality, but it is always possible that, through subsequent edits, an article could deteriorate in quality and accuracy. If later edits do reduce the quality of an article, it can be nominated for removal from the "featured article" list.

Most academics, librarians, and teachers do not consider Wikipedia to be a reliable or credible source. Though Wikipedia has shown that it can produce high-quality content, it can not be trusted to always post articles that are uniformly factual, neutral, complete, thorough, and accurate. However, despite its limitations, Wikipedia also has its merits. This highly innovative online encyclopedia revolutionized the recording of history by transforming it into a collaborative and digital activity. Wikipedia has transformed the way that we, as humans, create, share, exchange, debate, and preserve information. When used properly, as a starting point for research, Wikipedia can be both useful and informative.

TEN GREAT QUESTIONS

TO ASK A LIBRARIAN OR TEACHER

1 Where can I find accurate information from reputable online sources that are expert-written and -reviewed?

2 What prevents people from contributing deliberately false, fabricated, or inaccurate information to Wikipedia?

3 How much should I trust the information I find on Wikipedia?

4 How can I spot unreliable articles on Wikipedia?

5 How should I notify Wikipedia about an article's inaccuracy? Should I just correct the article myself?

6 Should I use Wikipedia as a cited source in my research paper?

7 What other types of resources would be considered more accurate or reliable?

8 What role, if any, should Wikipedia play in my research?

9 As both a site of learning and communication, is Wikipedia a safe environment for young people?

10 How can I verify the information I find on Wikipedia?

GLOSSARY

article A Wikipedia entry.

bias An inclination to look at something in a certain way.

bot Software applications that run automated tasks over the Internet.

collaborative Describing an effort by many people to work together in the creation of something.

controversial Describing issues that can cause division or disagreement between people.

dot-com company A company that does most of its business on the Internet.

editorial process All the stages of work that go into proofreading, correcting, enhancing, and polishing a piece of writing.

forum An online site where people can discuss topics in the form of posted messages.

IP address The numeric address of a computer on the Internet.

philosophy The general understanding of values and reality; the guiding principles by which one lives or works.

revenue The income that a company receives through its business activities.

revert To return to a former condition.

stub A Wikipedia article that contains only a few sentences and is too short to provide encyclopedic coverage of the subject.

vandalism The changing of the content of a Wikipedia article in order to deliberately compromise its integrity.

verifiable Capable of being confirmed or found truthful or accurate.

wiki Technology that allows the collaborative creation of Web pages and contributions of content from multiple users.

FOR MORE INFORMATION

Canadian Internet Project (CIP)
Ryerson University School of Radio and Television Arts
Toronto, ON M5B 2K3
Canada
(416) 979-5000, ext.7549
The CIP is a Ryerson University–based, long-running research project center-
ing on Internet usage, trends, attitudes, and many other factors in our
relationship with the Web.

Computer History Museum
1401 North Shoreline Boulevard
Mountain View, CA 94043
(650) 810-1010
Web site: http://www.computerhistory.org
The Computer History Museum is dedicated to exploring the development of
computer technology from the twentieth century through to the Internet
age and beyond.

Family Online Safety Institute (FOSI)
815 Connecticut Avenue, Suite 220
Washington, DC 20006
(202) 572-6252
Web site: http://www.fosi.org
The FOSI is an international, nonprofit organization that works to develop a
safer Internet for children and families. It works to influence public policies and educate the public.

Get Net Wise
Internet Education Foundation

1634 I Street NW
Washington DC 20009
Web site: http://www.getnetwise.org
Get Net Wise is part of the Internet Education Foundation, which works to
    provide a safe online environment for children and families.

International Technology Education Association (ITEA)
1914 Association Drive, Suite 201
Reston, VA 20191-1539
(703) 860-2100
Web site: http://www.iteaconnect.org
The ITEA promotes technology education and literacy.

Internet Keep Safe Coalition
1401 K Street NW, Suite 600
Washington, DC 20005
(866) 794-7233
Web site: http://www.ikeepsafe.org
The Internet Keep Safe Coalition is an educational resource for children and
    families that educates about Internet safety and ethics associated with
    Internet technologies.

The Internet Society (ISOC)
1775 Wiehle Avenue, Suite 201
Reston, VA 20190-5108
(703) 439-2120
Web site: http://www.isoc.org
The ISOC is a nonprofit organization that concentrates on maintaining high
    standards for Internet infrastructure and promotes education and govern-
    ment policies that promote open online environments.

i-SAFE Inc.
5900 Pasteur Court, Suite #100

Carlsbad, CA 92008
(760) 603-7911
Web site: http://www.isafe.org
Founded in 1998, i-SAFE Inc., is the leader in Internet safety education. Available in all fifty states, Washington, D.C., and Department of Defense schools located across the world, i-SAFE is a nonprofit foundation whose mission is to educate and empower youth to make their Internet experiences safe and responsible. The goal is to educate students on how to avoid dangerous, inappropriate, or unlawful online behavior.

Media Awareness Network
1500 Merivale Road, 3rd Floor
Ottawa, ON K2E 6Z5
Canada
(613) 224-7721
Web site: http://www.media-awareness.ca
The Media Awareness Network creates media literacy programs for young people. The site contains educational games about the Internet and media.

NetSmartz
Charles B. Wang International Children's Building
699 Prince Street
Alexandria, VA 22314-3175
(800) 843-5678
Web site: http://www.netsmartz.org
NetSmartz provides children, teens, and parents with resources to help educate young people about how to surf the Internet safely.

Open Source Initiative (OSI)
P.O. Box 410990, #256
San Francisco, CA 94114-0990

Web site: http://www.opensource.org
The OSI is actively involved in open source community-building, education, and public advocacy to promote awareness and the importance of nonproprietary software.

World Wide Web Consortium (W3C)
32 Vassar Street, Room 32-G515
Cambridge, MA 02139
Web site: http://www.w3.org
The W3C is the main international body that brings together many players to help set standards, technological and otherwise, for the Internet.

Web Sites

Due to the changing nature of Internet links, Rosen Publishing has developed an online list of Web sites related to the subject of this book. This site is updated regularly. Please use this link to access the list:

http://www.rosenlinks.com/dil/wiki

FOR FURTHER READING

Anderson, Jennifer Joline. *Wikipedia: The Company and Its Founders* (Technology Pioneers). Edina, MN: Essential Library, 2011.

Ayers, Phoebe, Charles Matthews, and Ben Yates. *How Wikipedia Works: And How You Can Be a Part of It*. San Francisco, CA: No Starch Press, 2008.

Bailey, Diane. *Cyber Ethics*. New York, NY: Rosen Central, 2008.

Barrett, Daniel J. *MediaWiki* (Wikipedia and Beyond). Sebastopol, CA: O'Reilly Media, 2008.

Brasch, Nicolas. *The Internet* (Technology Behind). Mankato, MN: Smart Apple Media, 2011.

Brown, Andrew. *A Brief History of Encyclopedias: From Pliny to Wikipedia* (Brief Histories). London, England: Hesperus Press, 2011.

Bruns, Axel. *Blogs, Wikipedia, Second Life, and Beyond* (Digital Formations). New York, NY: Peter Lang Publishing, 2008.

Dougherty, Terri. *Freedom of Expression and the Internet* (Hot Topics). Farmington Hills, MI: Greenhaven Press/Lucent Books, 2009.

Furgang, Kathy. *Netiquette: A Student's Guide to Digital Etiquette* (Digital and Information Literacy). New York, NY: Rosen Central, 2011.

Gaines, Ann Graham. *Ace Your Internet Research* (Ace It! Information Literacy). Berkeley Heights, NJ: Enslow Publishers, 2009.

O'Sullivan, Dan. *Wikipedia*. Burlington, VT: Ashgate Publishing, 2009.

Shaw, Maura D. *Mastering Online Research*. Cincinnati, OH: Writer's Digest Books, 2007.